Arise & Shine

Rochelle Fothergill

Published in London

ISBN: 9781527255012

Cover design: Daniel Ihediwa
Visit the author's website at www.rochellekrystal.com

Dedication

I would like to dedicate this book to dreamers. The contents of this book have been assembled together over the last few years and are combined with my teachings while doing missionary work and important lessons I have learned in my life. I believe this book will encourage and inspire the next generation. Any dream with a good cause is worth pursuing.

Contents

Acknowledgements

I would like to thank the people in my life who pushed and encouraged me to complete this book, especially my mother who has been a great help to me in this process.

A special thanks to Richard, Chantil, and Amnet Author Services for your support in editing.

Most importantly I would like to thank God for enabling me to write this book. I couldn't have done it without you!

Introduction

Dear Reader,

This book was written just for you.

It contains life-changing information in the form of stories, life experiences, and, most importantly, lessons and practical tools that can be applied daily to your life.

This book is a combined workbook that will enable you to practically apply the teachings to your life. Once you apply these lessons, the way you view yourself and the way you view life will change forever. For results to be seen you have to practice and apply what is taught. While you go through the book and complete the exercises, a better you is in the making. Take your time reading, embrace reflection, and embark on this new journey with excitement and expectation!

It's time to Arise & Shine. Will you?

Arise & shine, for your light has come.

— Isaiah 60:1

CHAPTER 1

Arise & Shine

Our deepest fear is not that we are inadequate. Our deepest fear is that we are powerful beyond measure. It is our light, not our darkness, that most frightens us. Your playing small does not serve the world. There is nothing enlightened about shrinking so that other people won't feel insecure around you. We are all meant to shine as children do. It's not just in some of us; it is in everyone. And as we let our own lights shine, we unconsciously give other people permission to do the same. As we are liberated from our own fear, our presence automatically liberates others.

— Marianne Williamson

Let your light shine

This is definitely one of my favourite quotes. It helps me to evaluate myself. What are my fears? What are my strengths? Why do I hold myself back in certain situations? How do I view myself? Am I useful to those around me or do I shy away in certain circumstances? How do others feel when they are around me? How is the world a better place because of me? I always ask myself these questions, and the answers are constant reminders that I am a work in progress. I am not perfect.

Letting your light shine inspires and liberates others. It encourages those around you to be their best and unique selves. When I see a person doing well, it encourages and motivates me to push myself and make improvements in my life.

You may be asking yourself, "What does it mean to shine?" and "How can I shine?"

Definition: **Shine**

- *"Give out a bright light."*
- *"Be very talented or perform very well."*
- *"A quality of brightness produced when light is reflected on something."*

A person who is shining is a person who radiates light and is operating to the best of their abilities. To shine, you need to be you at your best. Become all that you can be.

Everyone shines differently, so try not to compare your shine to someone else's. Rather, compare the effects of how you perform at your best, compared to when you're not performing as well as you could.

We are all a work in progress and are at different stages in our lives. We have our own race to run but, unfortunately, we look at our lives and compare where we are with where those around us are.

Picture where you want to be and what you want to achieve, let that desired outcome motivate and fuel you to reach your dreams and goals and ultimately to shine.

The destination is usually seen as the prize, but our life's journey is just as important. Remember, the skills and knowledge you have acquired are all for a purpose.

Exercise

First, to shine effectively, we need to recognise the things that are holding us back.

Are you able to identify the obstacles that are stopping you from achieving your goals?

Write down at least three things as they come to mind.

Example: I lack confidence in my ability to speak in public.

Three obstacles

1. ____

2. ____

3. ____

Now that your obstacles have been identified, go back and be more specific with your answers if you feel it's necessary. If not, just one word is fine if it adequately describes your challenge.

This time around, write down three solutions to the challenges you mentioned above. For example:

Solution—Find a job that involves public speaking.

Three practical solutions

1. ______________________________

____

2. ______________________________

____

3. ______________________________

____

Note that these practical solutions need to be clear, challenging and **implemented** for results to be seen.

Doing this exercise should bring clarity and you should see how making small changes to overcome your barriers can have a positive impact on your life.

Results are not always instant, it can take time. Be patient! Growth always follows, so be expectant!

It may feel weird pushing yourself out of your comfort zone and putting yourself in uncomfortable situations. However, like diamonds under pressure, that's when the beauty is seen and real transformation takes place.

This exercise will help you to become more solution focused and realise your potential. You are capable of achieving so much. Do not let fear prevent you from making progress.

What's your Outlook/Perspective in Life?

Every day when you wake up, you can consciously make a decision to shine. In order to shine effectively, you need to have a healthy outlook!

Let's look at the different definitions that are used to define one's outlook.

- "A habitual or characteristic mental attitude that determines how you will interpret and respond to situations."
- "The view or prospect from a particular place."
- "Prospect for the future: the political outlook."
- "The act or state of looking outward."

A young man's dream

Have you ever felt as if you were not good enough for your dream? Have you ever worked so hard for something you wanted? Only to be told that you don't have what it takes? Well, having a positive outlook can take you further than you could imagine.

Michael Jordan was fifteen years old when he got cut from his high school basketball team (his coach told him that he was not good enough). Michael was so distressed by the news that he cried when he got home.

However, instead of letting that cut deter Michael from pursuing his dream, he used this as motivation to train even harder than before.

When interviewed years later, Michael explained that whenever he was training and started to get tired or contemplated stopping, he would close his eyes and see the locker room list without his name on it. Upon seeing that list, he would find the drive and motivation he needed to keep training.

When faced with rejection and uncertainty, it's easy to quit when we hear "No" and give up. We think, "Oh I'm just not good enough, let me try something else." Sometimes we do not stick around long enough and pursue what we want to see if we can become better.

Despite the negative feedback from his coach, Michael decided that he was going to become good enough. He decided that he was going to be the best. It was a decision—a decision to become great. And it's one only you can make for yourself.

Michael Jordan knew that to be the best he would have to work and train harder than those around him. In his career, Michael Jordan made fourteen All-Star appearances. He earned six National Basketball Association (NBA) championships, and five NBA Most Valuable Player (MVP) titles. The ESPN TV channel also ranks him as being the number-one top North American Athlete of the twentieth century.

If ever you feel like giving up, think about Michael Jordan's story. What's your perspective when the odds are not in your favour? What would you have done if you were in Michael's situation?

There have been times when I've felt inadequate. I've questioned my abilities and asked myself "Who am I to be doing this?" But I have had to remind myself that I should never limit what I can achieve because of how I feel or even because of my abilities. Whatever it is that you want to achieve, find ways to work towards it and continuously improve yourself.

Six keys to help you have a better outlook

Key 1: Maintain a positive outlook when you're going through testing times.

When unforeseen circumstances arise, and situations do not turn out as expected, how do you respond?

Do you blame others, yourself, or even God?

Challenging times are difficult, but we grow and develop as a person when we face obstacles and tough situations. What I am saying is that when you are going through something that is difficult and challenging, you can be mindful of how to use that situation to become better and to help you grow as a person.

Could it be that certain trials and tests serve as fuel to push us and from them, we can learn valuable life lessons? They enable us to gain skills that we may not have acquired had we not gone through challenges.

Every time you face an obstacle in life, it forces you to use your imagination and think outside the box. Therefore, learn to view your situations from different perspectives, not as obstacles but rather as part of a learning curve.

For example, when I was younger, I found myself applying for one particular job and after four attempts I finally was offered an interview.

When applying the fourth time, I asked myself, "Why did I not get a response the last three times?" It dawned on me that I hadn't put enough time or effort into the failed applications. With the fourth application, I took my time and tried my very best, and I was offered an interview. If I hadn't stopped to ask myself "Why," I would not have put that extra effort in and I may not have been offered the job.

Can you see how a shift in perspective can make a difference to an outcome? Instead of focusing on the failed attempts, I used my time and energy to focus on what I could do to improve my application, which then resulted in a successful outcome.

In life, you will find yourself in situations and circumstances that you cannot change. However, what you can do is choose how you react towards them.

The way you react to your circumstances is important as the long-term effects of your actions will either work for you or against you.

For example, in times of hardships and stress when looking for a way to escape your current situation, taking drugs and drinking may seem harmless. However, in the long term, it can be destructive and lead to addiction and even homelessness. You may think that will never happen to you, but no one intentionally sets out to become homeless, neither do they purposely choose to become addicted to drugs.

Our reactions can lead to destructive behaviour if we don't look ahead and think about the consequences.

Facing difficulties is inevitable, learning from them is optional.

— John Maxwell

Key 2: Reach out.

In times of trouble reach out and talk to those around you. People who care about you will want to help or just listen if they know that will assist you. Reaching out, talking or releasing your feelings is very important as the first step in this process.

Confide in those you trust such as family and friends as keeping emotions bottled in is unhealthy and can be damaging to your mental health and physical state.

Key 3: Never give up, regardless of your obstacles.

A man on a mission

On a hot summer's day, an excited young man was stuck in an airport in Puerto Rico. He was on his way to catch a plane to the British Virgin Islands for a date with a beautiful young lady he had recently met.

An unexpected announcement in the airport had been made, and to the young man's surprise, his flight had been cancelled. Shocked and confused, the young man paused to think, "Cancelling this date is not an option and I'm not waiting for the next flight."

He walked up and down the airport thinking to himself "What can I do?" The young man then came across a pilot who had a private plane and agreed to take him to his destination at the agreed price of $500.

Unbeknown to the pilot, the young man was thinking, "I don't have five hundred dollars," but he left, informing the pilot that he'll be back soon. The young man wrote on a piece of cardboard "$39 to the British Virgin Islands" and stood in the airport with this sign.

Very soon, some of those who were booked on the same cancelled flight as the young man started to approach him. The young man managed to fill the seats on the plane he'd hired and raised more than the $500 initially requested by the pilot and, shortly thereafter, made his way to meet his date.

The end

Would you have done this if your flight was cancelled?

The young man in this story is known as Sir Richard Branson, multibillionaire and the owner of Virgin airlines.

The vital message in this story is that Richard did not give up. He saw a challenge in front of him, but he did not view it as an obstacle but rather as an opportunity that allowed him to use his imagination.

What I love about Richard's story is not just that he got to see his crush, but that the circumstance he found himself in was what gave him the idea to start his own company. It turns out, the situation he found himself "stuck" in was, in fact, an opportunity.

Well, that's how ***he*** saw it.

In life, we may face events that look like setbacks, and maybe for a while, do set us back. Ultimately, these setbacks can lead to greater things depending on how we view and respond to them. Some of the most successful people in history were faced with obstacles that forced them to work harder than before. Though it was tough, they came out on top.

Here are some examples, of people who had faced failure and rejection many times before seeing the fruits of their labour.

- Abraham Lincoln ran for office several times before he became president.

- Henry Ford's early businesses failed and left him with little money on five occasions before he founded his successful motor company.

- Oprah Winfrey lost her first anchor job because her employers thought that she got "emotionally invested" in her stories. She then went on to run her own show, which became the highest-rated daytime American talk show. Did I mention Oprah runs her own production company? Oh, and she's a billionaire, too.

- Harland David Sanders (founder of KFC) had his famous chicken recipe rejected 1,009 times before he made it big.

- Walt Disney was fired by a newspaper editor because he "lacked imagination and had no good ideas." There are now several Disney theme parks across the world, and his company is one of the most powerful and influential in media history.

- Thomas Edison was told in his early years by his teachers that he was "too stupid to do anything." Even when it came to inventing, Edison made a thousand unsuccessful attempts before successfully inventing the light bulb.

All these people faced trials and difficult times.

For them, there was no "plain sailing"—their roads were continuously rocky, and life must have been harder than they'd imagined.

But they stuck to it. They kept going. They pushed through the barriers and did not let rejection deter them from the course they had in mind.

One of the things that separate successful people from ordinary people is that successful people do not stop until they achieve their desired goals.

Key 4: Ask yourself—Where do I see myself going?

Will you allow the situations you find yourself in to define who you are, or where you are going in life?

No matter what you have been through, you can do anything you put your mind to. Do not limit yourself!

What profession do you want to go into? What type of person do you want to become?

The answer and the fulfilment of those questions are dependent upon you.

As a teenager, I was quiet and very shy. I was aware of this and wanted to become more confident. I was confident only at home and wanted to be like this even around people outside my family.

I decided to do something practical and take Drama as a GCSE subject. This was not because I wanted to get out of writing-based classes, (well, partly!) but because I realised that if I pushed myself to do the things I was uncomfortable with, it will enable me to become far more confident.

As a result of taking Drama GCSE, my confidence and self-esteem grew, and I became comfortable acting in front of others. Years later, my confidence skyrocketed. I picked challenging job roles, and I placed myself in more uncomfortable situations where I had to teach, preach, and lead on projects with various people.

When I first started teaching, I was nervous even with small crowds. However, I always pushed myself and so did those around me. Over time, I began to see the positive changes and those around me would say, "I've noticed you are a lot more confident than you used to be!"

Consequently, by putting myself in uncomfortable situations, I felt better about myself and my abilities. Today, I can speak confidently in front of large audiences!

Whatever it is in life you want to do, you first have to believe that you ***can*** do it. And if you don't believe in yourself, find someone who does so that they can motivate and push you until you do start to believe.

Secondly, you have to be prepared to work for what you want. This means stepping out of your comfort zone and pushing yourself until you start to see the desired results despite how you feel.

Great things don't come out from comfort zones.

— Anonymous

Key 5: Steps to improve yourself.

Treat others well

Treat others how you want them to treat you. You have probably heard the saying, "Do not treat people based on how they treat you." Your standard should always be higher.

Show gratitude

Show appreciation when people do something to help you, no matter how small. People like being around those who are positive and show gratitude.

I did not realise it at the time but, while doing missionary work, I could recall someone praising me and my team. He was touched and felt valued because we celebrated the small things he did, and showed appreciation for things that most people would look over. Showing appreciation, therefore, can impact someone's life beyond our imagination.

Push yourself out of your comfort zone

You will become a better person in the process and will also learn new skills that you're likely to use throughout your life.

Try new things

You could find your passion in doing something you have never tried before. As you begin to explore, allow your mind and life experiences to expand.

Goals

It's important to write your goals down, but it's also essential to have challenging ones.

Dr Gali Matthews experimented with over 625 participants, which included bankers, entrepreneurs, artists, and lawyers.

Matthews found that those who wrote down their goals and dreams regularly had a significantly higher success rate at accomplishing their goals and dreams compared to those who did not.

Seeing what you want to achieve regularly will motivate and push you to succeed.

SMART Goals

Goal-setting is important but making them SMART helps to make the goal more achievable and will give you vision and direction. Smart goals can be defined as specific, measurable goals that can be completed in a particular time frame.

S—Strategic and specific
M—Measurable
A—Attainable
R—Realistic/relevant
T—Time-bound

Strategic and specific

It is important that your goals are strategic and specific—by asking yourself the "WH" questions, you will be able to do this more effectively.

What: What is it that I want to achieve?
Why: Why do I want to achieve it?
Who: Who is involved in the achievement of this goal?
Where: Is there a location?
Which: Is there anything specific I need to achieve this goal? Are there any obstacles I could face when setting out to accomplish this goal?

Here is a good example of a specific goal.

Within six months—by (date) I would like to pass my driving test because I want the freedom and ease to travel whenever I want.

This goal clearly identifies when you want to achieve it, what you want to accomplish, and addresses your motivations behind the goal.

Measurable

Measurability in goal setting allows you to measure and track the progress that you are making in attaining your goal.

For example, a person who sets out to lose one stone in two months can see whether they are on track in reaching this target by measuring how much they've lost (which represents their progress) with how much time they have left to lose the weight.

Attainable

Setting attainable goals allows you to set goals that you can reach. It is important to set goals that aren't too hard; otherwise, they may seem unreachable, and this could demotivate you. Also, goals that are too easy will not challenge you and won't give you fulfilment.

Having an attainable goal means that you have or can easily access the resources you need to achieve your goal.

Realistic/Relevant

When setting goals, they should be realistic so that they can be achieved. For example, setting a goal to learn how to play the piano within the next three months may be unrealistic if you have upcoming exams and are already juggling various activities. Setting a goal should also be relevant to areas in your life where you want to see improvement. Is learning to play the piano relevant to what you want to do in the immediate future?

It's important to evaluate your life so you know if you can reach the expectations that you've placed upon yourself. Is there enough time to do this in my schedule? Will I have enough energy to take on a new project? Will I make time?

Time-bound

Setting a goal with a specific time frame and date helps to create urgency and focus. Taking this a step further involves breaking the goal down into chunks; this will enable you to track/monitor what has been done. By having a deadline, you will be able to assess whether you're on track to achieve your goal or whether you are behind and need to make changes.

Who are you accountable to?

Role models and mentors

Research your role models, learn what they have done to get to where they are now, and do the same. Role models and mentors are out there, but it's vital to have good ones! People you can learn from and who want to see you succeed. Those who have your best interest at heart are people worth being around. So, find them! Research and study those whom you want to be like because that's how you become better.

Are there people in your circle that could potentially mentor you? List two or three names and approach them this week. If you do not have any, be active in finding one.

1. ______________________________

2. ______________________________

3. ______________________________

Key 6: Feed yourself good food!

Our life's course is determined by what penetrates our hearts.

Our minds play a crucial role in our everyday lives, as this is where our thoughts and actions stem from. It is vital that we feed our minds with healthy things.

The books we read, the TV programs we watch, the music we listen to, and the conversations we have will somehow influence us. So, it is important that we monitor what we are influenced by. For example, consistently **watching programs** with people gossiping, hanging around gossipers, and **reading** books filled with gossip is bound to have a negative effect on your mind. This illustrates that our mind can be influenced by what enters it, consequently, our thoughts can lead to negative actions such as gossiping about people.

We all have a choice about how we act and respond to situations. You may be in a situation that you cannot control; however, there are certain things we can control and should be mindful of.

There may be activities that you enjoy doing, and even friends that you like being around, but over time they may show to be toxic in your life. Be vigilant about what and who you allow in your life, as certain things can hold you back, and certain people can pull you down.

Ultimately, the question you should ask yourself is, "Are these things/ people helping me to become a better person?"

If I was to eat at McDonald's every day, I might not see the effects instantly, but after a while, I sure would! Our actions may gratify us at the time, but the consequences of them soon catch up with us!

Our actions tend to follow our thoughts, so be aware of which thoughts you choose to entertain.

After reading these steps, what can you do practically to become a better person?

List three things that you could improve on, and steps as to how you will do this.

1. ______________________________

____

____

____

2. ______________________________

____

____

____

3. ______________________________

____

____

____

Chapter Summary

- Whatever you feed yourself with, will align with your thinking.
- When the outcome is not what you expected, ask yourself what actions are required to create positive changes.
- Try not to focus on the negative, but instead focus on the good in the situation and be grateful for what you have. Not every situation that we find ourselves in will be positive, but our subsequent actions can have life-changing effects.
- Your struggles are often the pathways that lead you to your success.
- Be led by your positive thoughts and not your negative ones.

Summarise the key points you found in this chapter

Key 🗝

Key 🗝

Key 🗝

Key 🗝

Key 🗝

Potential is never what you've done, it's always what you could do but haven't done yet.

— Unknown

CHAPTER 2

Purpose & Passion

Purpose can be described as:

- *"The reason for which something exists or is done."*
- *"The object for which one strives or for which something exists; an aim or a goal."*

Passion can be described as:

- *"An extreme interest in, or wish to do, something."*
- *"Something that is desired intensely."*

Live intentionally

You cannot live on purpose without a plan. One of my favourite motivational speakers, Brian Tracy, said, "*A genius without a road map will get lost in any country, but an average person with a road map will find their way to any destination.*"

In essence, a person with goals and a plan of action on how to achieve those goals is going to be more productive and has a greater chance of achieving their dreams, compared to someone who goes with the flow and hopes for the best. Hoping for the best will get you somewhere, but planning for the best is more likely to get you to your intended destination.

If there's a goal and a plan of action on how to achieve it, we're likely to see it through and accomplish it because that is where our focus is. You may find that setting out to achieve something does not always go to plan, and may not be "smooth sailing." However, by having a guideline on how and when you need to complete a goal or a project, you will make it more achievable.

Take a look at buildings, for example, before they are made there's a plan of action put in place, from constructing a layout to laying the foundations and building a structure.

By developing a plan, everyone knows what their job is and how to carry it out. Planning, therefore, provides clarity and vision. Building and working towards what you want in life may take longer than anticipated, but having a plan in place will help you to get the job done effectively.

What's the purpose of your plan? You need to know the purpose of a building before you build it.

We all want our lives to mean something and to stand for a purpose, but if we don't know what that something is, how can we be purposeful in our approach?

When people say to me, "I don't know what my purpose is, I don't know what to do with my life." I ask them, "what are your passions, what makes you smile, what would you do if money was not a problem?"

Ask yourself these questions, and think about your responses.

When you know the answer to these questions, you'll find that it's easier to find purpose because you've identified your passions.

Purpose and passion are connected, so we'll take a look at passion shortly.

Let's look at your goals!

Do you know that you are 42 per cent more likely to achieve a goal if it's written down?

This is because the mind is more conscious of what it can see, and subconsciously works to obtain those things. So, writing down what you want to achieve and do, plays a vital part in helping you to achieve your goals.

What three SMART goals would you like to achieve within the next three months? For example: learn how to play the saxophone, achieving top grades in your exams, pass a driving test, or completing a 10k race.

Exercise

Top three goals

1. ______________________________

____

2. ______________________________

____

3. ______________________________

____

Now that we've identified your top three goals for the next three months, we need to break this down.

Month one

What three things can you focus on in month one?

1. ______________________________

____

2. ______________________________

____

3. ______________________________

____

Month two

What three things can you focus on in month two?

1. ______________________________

____

2. ______________________________

____

3. ______________________________

____

Month three

What three things can you focus on in month three?

1. ______________________________

____

2. ______________________________

____

3. ______________________________

____

Some of the examples I have mentioned above may seem simple. Consider this, if there's no plan of action behind these goals, for example when and how you will achieve them, then how will you accomplish more complex goals? It may take you up to a year to do something, simply because you kept putting it off. **Take charge of your life, try not to put off things that can be done today until tomorrow because time waits for no one!**

Your purpose is often linked to your passions, and your passions are usually connected to your talents.

Let's take a look at finding your passions.

We excel in the things we're passionate about

When you are passionate about something, you are more likely to succeed in that thing and obtain better results compared to doing something that does not motivate you.

For instance, I majored in psychology and counselling at university. I loved the subject, and found it fascinating yet challenging. I believe that I did well in my major because I was passionate about the subject and interested in the modules I chose. Looking back on my journey in education, I find that I have achieved better results in subjects that I enjoyed. I can also say the same for my work experience. I've stayed in the jobs I've enjoyed for longer and have put more effort into them.

When you are passionate about a cause, it's easier to excel because that passion comes from a place that drives you forward. Have you ever met a person who was successful in something they didn't enjoy? It's easier to excel in things that we are passionate about compared to things we have no passion for.

That passion will wake you up early in the morning to start you training for that 10k race. That same passion will keep you up all night preparing you for an exam.

It's passion that pushes us to become who we need to be!

Why settle for a life of mediocrity when you can live a life full of purpose? Do things that excite and challenge you. If it does not challenge you, ask yourself, "Is it worth pursuing?"

Whatever venture or career you choose to take, make sure it's something you are passionate about. Don't just do it for the money or out of convenience.

Exercise

What are your passions?

Write down three things that you're passionate about.

Passion 1.

Passion 2.

Passion 3.

What are the driving forces behind these passions?

Driving force 1.

Driving force 2.

Driving force 3.

How will these passions be executed?

Action 1.

Action 2.

Action 3.

Discuss with someone close to you how you could make these passions a reality. Add a time scale to it and an action plan of how you will achieve it—make them SMART!

They say the richest place on earth is the grave because in it are ideas and dreams, books that were never written and inventions and cures that were never made.

— Les Brown

The world doesn't just want the gifts you have to share; the world needs them.

— Unknown

Do not die with your passions, share them with the world and live your life to the fullest.

You may be asking yourself, "What if I don't know what my passions are? What if I don't know what I want to do in life?" Can I suggest that you **try new things**? This will help to expand your experiences, develop new skills and will give you a feel for what you enjoy doing.

When I was younger, I wanted to be everything under the sun. As I grew older, I was unsure of what I wanted to do and I found myself pursuing various things. Being open and trying new experiences enabled me to learn new skills, equipped me to face various situations, helped me to be more confident under pressure and enabled me to develop my people skills.

By taking this approach, you may find yourself doing things you would never have contemplated, and you may find that you love one of them!

Working with young people was never on my list of things to do, but I decided to try something different, and have found it so rewarding. I was able to encourage and mentor young people and help them realise their potential. Yes, it had its challenges, but I grew tremendously from those challenges and, as a result, developed into the confident person I am today.

Give it time, you may not know what you want to do for a while, and that's okay—you don't have to have everything figured out.

As you grow and mature, you will experience new things, and your desires and dreams may be different than they use to be. Also, your outlook may change and what was once important to you may seem less so over time.

Your passions will push you into a life full of purpose

When you're passionate about something, you're all in. The best salespeople, or the best athletes, for example, are excellent at what they do because they give 110 per cent. When a person gives 110 per cent they can't help but excel in life

A person who is passionate about what they do does not need to be woken up in the morning, because their pursuits drive them out of bed. Living a life full of purpose requires dedication and hard work

Usher, the successful pop and R&B singer, knew that he would become famous when he realised what he wanted to do

At the tender age of fourteen, when Usher first started working with his mentor, he was exposed to the kind of life he could live. However, he was not distracted by the things that came along with fame but focused on pursuing his dream. He spent most of his time in the studio making music and made an effort to be around people who he admired

To date, Usher's accolades include eight Grammy awards, eighteen Billboard Music Awards, nine Soul Train Music Awards, eight American Music Awards, seven Teen Choice Awards, and the list goes on!

The reason behind Usher's great accomplishments is that he had a vision for his life and this was accompanied with passion; I'm sure that this is what enabled Usher to pursue his dreams with hard work and diligence.

Trials will come to test your dreams

In life, we say we want things—good grades, a successful business, a house, and so on; however, when times get tough and obstacles come your way, you have to keep pushing to fight for what you want. The people you see in the limelight on TV in music shows and in general those who are successful, all fought until they saw their dreams become a reality. As mentioned earlier, anything that's worth pursuing will have its challenges. We all make plans, but life does not always go to plan, so it's important that you do not give up. Instead, work hard and smart, to achieve the plans you have.

A life of service

The real power lies in service to others.

— Cheryl Bachelder

Life's most persistent and urgent question is: What are you doing for others?

— Martin Luther King Jr.

You are not here merely to make a living. You are here in order to enable the world to live more amply, with greater vision, with a finer spirit of hope and achievement. You are here to enrich the world and you impoverish yourself if you forget the errand.

— Woodrow T. Wilson

The individuals who said these quotes learned from their life experiences that through serving others, life becomes more fulfilling, enriching, and meaningful. Serving puts the way we see things into perspective and enables us to find our passions. These great leaders demonstrated that when a life of service is lived, the effects of it transcend their lifetime, and can affect the generations to come.

Some of the most influential people who lived on this earth were known for their service to others—for example, Mother Teresa, Eleanor Roosevelt, Malcolm X. They did not live for themselves but rather for a cause.

Take a look at Nelson Mandela, for example. He was a young lawyer who had things going for him, but there was a cause that he fought for (the ending of apartheid in South Africa) that resulted in him being incarcerated for twenty-seven years. What he fought for was not just about himself, it was greater than him as this cause affected a nation.

In what ways can you help your community?

When we choose selfless acts like giving back, we are making the world a better place.

I have found that my life is more fulfilling when I am doing things that I am passionate about while in service to others. In my short life, I have had the pleasure of working with young people, and my experience of working with them has enabled me to mentor, advise, teach, and counsel. This experience has been rewarding for me as I can see the difference that serving another person can make. It has also shown me that what I say can empower others and positively affect their choices for years to come.

It may be hard to think far ahead but know that your life is more than just you. Your children are going to be affected by how you live your life and so will their children.

Ask yourself these two crucial questions—what type of person do I want to become, and what do I want to be known for?

Exercise

Write down three things that you would like to be known for, for making the world a better place. These will become your three life visions.

Your answers to these questions are necessary, as your goals will direct the decisions you make in life, which will determine your focus.

1. ______________________________

____

____

2. ______________________________

____

____

3. ______________________________

____

____

Living life without limits

Consult not your fears but your hopes and your dreams. Think not about your frustrations, but about your unfilled potential. Concern yourself not with what you tried and failed in, but with what is still possible for you to do.

— Pope John XXIII

YOU, yes you, have so much potential within you. It's important you know that the only limits you have are the ones you place upon yourself.

What are the limits that you have placed upon yourself due to **fear**? Is it fear of failing or fear of the unknown?

Below are some examples of common fears that hold people back:

Fear of rejection—Not applying to a university because you fear you'll be rejected.

Lack of trust—You may have grown up facing rejection, and, as a result, you don't trust people. So, you expect others to reject you.

Fear of others' opinions—You may hold yourself back and hesitate to express your opinions because you want to fit. You may be afraid of going against the norm, so you copy your friends even when they do things you don't agree with.

Exercise

Whatever it is that you feel is holding you back, slowing you down, or hindering you from moving forward, write it down below.

With each point think deeply, and ask yourself—how did that become a limitation?

Where did this fear come from?

What is the root of this fear?

What measures can I put in place to overcome these limitations, fears, and worries?

It may mean discussing these points with someone close to you, with a view to overcoming them. There are few "quick fixes" in life, but through specific action and wise counsel, you can overcome the fear of the things that are holding you back.

Limit 1.

Limit 2.

Limit 3.

We have all been labelled by others, whether positive or negative. It is so important not to limit yourself in spite of what people have said and what others have done to you.

From time to time, feelings of fear and inadequacy may come. As you become aware of their frequency, you can learn how to ignore and dismiss such limiting thought patterns. Instead, make a choice to replace negative thoughts with positive ones. Having a positive, can-do mind-set, will increase your confidence and give you the boost you need to get things done.

Don't allow past mistakes to be a barrier stopping you from doing what you would like to do. Instead, allow your past to be the stepping stone to your future success. Many successful people would not be where they are today if it wasn't for their past failures and mistakes. **It's from our failings that we learn how to succeed.** You can choose to learn from your experiences, and, as a result, grow into a wiser and better-equipped person.

As well as this, it's important that we are around people that want to see us succeed. There are two types of people: those who push you and cheer you on, and those who crush your dreams and speak negative words into your life. Be careful who you confide in, and surround yourself with positive people. If you don't have friends around to encourage and motivate you, become your own cheerleader.

Some of you have friends and even close family members who have knocked down your confidence. You've been told that your dreams are too big, you're not smart enough, you don't have what it takes but, despite what you hear, keep going anyway—you've got a purpose to fight for!

Purpose and passion are interconnected

Nelson Mandela and Martin Luther King lived a life full of purpose because they had a passion for what they fought for. In turn, they left their mark on this earth.

There are many people, such as inventors and human activists, who have left legacies through various means. Here are some examples:

Jesus Christ—Spiritual teacher, the central figure of Christianity

Steve Jobs—Cofounder of Apple, known for his creativity and innovative products

Martin Luther King—Civil rights leader

Nelson Mandela—Anti-apartheid leader, president of South Africa

Princess Diana—Humanitarian

Marcus Aurelius—Roman emperor and philosopher

Mother Teresa—Missionary

All these people have something in common—their contribution made a lasting impact throughout the world in a positive way.

Don't let your age deter you from becoming who you want to become. You're neither too young nor too old to start dreaming. No matter where you are in life, it's never too late to pursue your dreams.

Most people, if not all who have become successful, faced many setbacks and even failed along the way. However, they were able to meet with success because they never gave up, so don't let failure or age deter you from your pursuits.

The best way to predict the future is to create it.

— Abraham Lincoln

In a TED talk called "Trusting your struggle," Zain Asher shared her story of working in local news. Her dream was to work for CNN and she also desired to work in international news.

Zain wanted to get into business news so desperately that she taught herself various topics in that field. She did not have any interviews lined up, but she knew that she had to be prepared for the day an opportunity came.

After years of studying, Zain came across the business news executive of CNN, and—you guessed it—he needed a reporter. Zain managed to land herself an interview, and it's not surprising that the interview was a success. Zain was so well prepared that, even though she had no experience in that field, she was offered a reporter's job on the spot! Zain mentioned a phrase that was crucial to her attitude. *"Success comes when opportunity meets preparation."*

While giving her talk, Zain explained that her older brother taught her to prepare well before that crucial interview.

That brother is Chiwetel Ejiofor who, at a young age, dreamed of becoming an actor. Aged thirteen, he started to learn how to memorise scripts and studied a variety of plays. He even wrote Shakespeare on his wall. Even if he didn't have an audition coming up, he was always preparing for one—always preparing for what he dreamed of doing.

At the age of nineteen, he was cast by Steven Spielberg in a film called *Mustard*. Chiwetel has gone on to star in various films and has won various prestigious awards, including an Olivier for Best Actor in 2008.

From Zain and Chiwetel's experiences, we learn that hard work and preparation precedes success.

What separates great people from ordinary people?

- Work ethic—Are you willing to put in time and effort even when you do not feel like it to achieve desired results?
- Mind-set—"*A man without a vision will perish*" (Prov. 29:18). Know what it is you want to achieve and stay focused until you see it come into fruition.

Whatever it is that you want to do or become, prepare now—don't wait for the opportunity to arise. When an opportunity arises, you are more likely to succeed if you are prepared; more so than if you are just talented.

Chapter Summary

- To have a life full of purpose, one must live intentionally (take ownership of your life).
- You are more likely to fulfil your goals when there is a passion and a meaningful cause behind them.
- You are full of potential.
- Live life without limitations.
- The only limits that exist are the ones you place upon yourself.
- Your life is more than just you—live it to the full, leave a legacy, and die empty.
- "Your successes are made out of the ingredients of your struggles."
  — T. D. Jakes

Summarise the key points you found in this chapter

Key 🗝

Key 🗝

Key 🗝

Key 🗝

Key 🗝

There is no passion to be found playing small, in settling for a life that is less than the one you are capable of living.

— Nelson Mandela

CHAPTER 3

Labels

Remove the unwanted labels

Labelling can be described as "the process of attaching a descriptive word to something or someone." It is a belief given to someone based on perception or stereotype. The theory suggests that people behave in ways that are a reflection of how others have labelled them; these typically are negative labels. In turn, the individual is likely to accept the label that has been placed upon them and will see themselves as deviant. The term deviant can be described as the behaviour that strays away from society's accepted norms. As a result, the individual is likely to act in ways that fulfil the expectations of those labels.

Here is a story demonstrating deviant behaviour. A young girl lived a troubled childhood. Born to parents who were both alcoholics; not knowing her father- who was a rapist and given up by her young mother was only the start. The young girl was subsequently adopted by her grandparents who also had their own issues.

By the age of 11 the young girl started to engage in sexual activities at school in exchange for food, cigarettes and drugs. By the age of 14 the young girl discovered she was pregnant, she soon after dropped out of school and was forced to give her baby up for adoption. As she grew up, she became more promiscuous and led a life of prostitution. Her name is Aileen Wuornos, and unfortunately, she found fame as a serial killer.

Aileen's story is quite intense, isn't it?

If you were to guess what became of this lady after hearing about her childhood, you would have probably said something negative, right?

Think about Aileen's childhood, what labels do you think were given to her as she grew up?

So, is this theory true? Do we become what society expects of us? In many instances, individuals do live up to the expectations that have been placed upon them by society. It's sad, but society will look at a person's past and label them. Some labels have been placed on others by society and may be necessary for the interest of the public. For example, labelling a person based on the crime they have committed warns society of the threats that a person may pose. But regardless of the labels placed upon us, despite our past mistakes and experiences, our actions and experiences don't define who we will become.

Well let's look at another example:

At the age of nine, a girl was raped; by ten years of age, she was molested by two close family members. She became pregnant at the age of fourteen years and kept this a secret for seven months until the day her baby was delivered. However, the baby was prematurely born and died as a result of complications. Her younger sister was given up for adoption, and she lost her brother to AIDS.

By the age of fourteen, her mother wanted her out of the house due to her unruly behaviour and took her to a detention home. When they arrived, the mother was told that there was not enough room for her and that she should return in two weeks. At this point, the young girl's mother suggested that she live with her father. Shortly after losing her baby, during a conversation, her dad told her, "this is your second chance, this is your opportunity to seize this moment and make something of your life." And that's what she did, she became the world's richest TV presenter, and has helped so many people along her journey. Her name is Oprah Winfrey.

From looking at Oprah's experiences what labels do you think Oprah received?

There are individuals who despite what others have said, and regardless of what they have been through, have chosen to reject the labels that others placed upon them. The two females above have very similar stories;

one could say that Oprah had good advice from her dad, which helped her realise she had the choice to turn her life around. Whereas, Aileen was abandoned by her mother and may not have had sound advice whilst growing up. Many different reasons come into play when assessing an individual's choice, but what did one lady do that the other did not?

Well, instead of becoming a product of her environment and her past life experiences, Oprah rejected the labels that society had placed upon her and took the positive advice that was given to her. This isn't at all an easy thing to do, as life's circumstances affect us in different ways and we all have different coping mechanisms. We don't have control over our past, but we can plan our future. Both cases are different and have varying factors, but despite this, a choice was one thing they both had in common. You also have a choice to make.

These two examples are quite profound, but there are many people who can identify with some aspects of those stories.

Despite what people may say about you, you don't have to become a product of your environment. People may look at your life and may label you based upon the area you were brought up in. You may be surrounded by crime, drugs, poverty, prostitution and abusive people but you don't have to become and do these things. I'm not minimising what a person goes through, or saying it's easy but I am highlighting the aspect of choice. Truth is some people don't know any better and have adopted destructive behaviours and are not sure how to get out of them. But it's never too late to make a change and seek help from professionals such as counsellors, therapists, family, and friends who have your best interest.

Like Oprah, despite facing opposition there are many people who have come out of their situations and used that as a drive to empower those around them, make something of themselves and pursue their dreams. Look at Christiano Ronaldo—a famous footballer—his family suffered immensely with financial difficulties. However, despite this, he went on to become one of the best footballers of our time.

Yusef Salaam at the age of fifteen was imprisoned for just under seven years for assault and rape—a crime he didn't commit and was later exonerated for. Yusef Salaam is now an author, public speaker, entrepreneur, and advocate for social justice. How is it that these people despite their environments and challenging upbringings have managed to make a positive impact on society?

In our everyday life, we have all had experiences where those close to us have labelled us, such as parents, teachers, and friends. Without even knowing it, at times, we also label ourselves.

Despite what you go through, there comes a point when you have to take ownership of your life. These labels may have been hurtful and may have even left you with some scars, so it may mean getting extra help such as seeking counselling, mentorship, or therapy to help deal with this. But, taking the first step shows that you can move forward. Though society labels us and puts us in boxes, the truth is we can reject those labels and decide our own course. To reject something is simply not to accept it. Regardless of what others have said, choose today not to accept negative labels. You may not have succeeded in a few things, but that doesn't define you. Your past is your past and you can't change that. But what you can change is how you respond to that past and the success you pursue thereafter, despite the challenges you may face.

Forgiveness is key—I've been wronged by people and hurt many times. The only way I was able to move forward was by forgiving those who hurt me. Doing this does not take away what they have done, but it sure frees you up from emotions of bitterness and resentment. Forgiveness is for your own benefit as it helps you to move on with your life. Putting these suggestions into practice is easier said than done!

Have you ever heard of the saying "Your test will become your testimony?" This saying is so true because whatever you go through, you can learn from and, in turn, help those around you.

It could be in terms of giving advice, mentoring, or maybe starting an organisation that helps others with the same thing that you have been through.

Know that you have a story and whatever you have been through can help, encourage, and inspire someone else. In life, we do not always get our own way, and when things happen to us, we will not see the full picture, as we can only see what's in front of us.

But have you ever found looking back on some situations in your life that somehow, they have added strength to you.

The person who dumped you. The teacher who said you would never achieve that grade. The "friend" who always belittled you and betrayed your trust.

What you may not have seen down the road was that just maybe the person really was not for you. Indirectly, that teacher gave you the drive to work extra hard, and that "friend" had to go because all she/he was doing was bringing you down.

What seems at first as a negative, in the end, can turn out to be positive.

Progress is usually on the other end of action

Below are interviews of two people who, despite their past, are trying to be the best people they possibly can be.

Leah is twenty-five years old and works in the music profession. Her dream is to bring creatives together and promote great music.

Leah: When I was younger, I liked music and wanted to sing. When I got older, I realised I was a powerhouse and had the ability to do so much. The labels that others tried to place on me affected me because I was known to be a loud person, and I guess being compared to quieter people did make me quiet at times. Now I embrace myself, and others who have the same qualities are drawn to me.

As I grew up, I started to care less about the opinions that did not serve me and the expectations that those around me held. I kept focused, did what I loved—which is music—and tried to be the best in my field. Over time, what I can say has changed, is getting to know myself, my strengths and weaknesses.

Carmen is twenty-one and works in the banking sector. She aspires to have an established successful career and to be happily married with children.

Carmen: I would describe my upbringing as somewhat disorderly. My past experiences and my future are my motivations and drive in life. I think the image one has of oneself is ever-changing but I believe as a whole you grow to understand yourself more. You gain an understanding of your emotions and behaviours, and actually know the reasons why you are built the way you are. I think as you learn about yourself more, you come to accept who and what you are. When you're younger, because there's a lot you don't know, I think it's easy to dislike yourself. But with age comes clarity and maturity and with that comes acceptance.

I believe it can be hard to determine whether or not someone's labels affect you immediately. I see myself as a relatively strong person, regardless of what people say about me or the labels they place on me. I am not defined by what people say; I define myself. If I have lived up to what someone thought of me, it's because I wanted to. I tend to disregard people's views of me a lot because it's irrelevant—if you're not helping me, you're hindering me. Life is too short to let that affect you, so it's with that belief that I reject people's opinions.

I'm forward thinking and, ultimately, I aim for everything I do to add towards my future.

The accounts of these two young ladies show that despite what others have said and in spite of their upbringings, they are focusing on their futures and have embraced the women that they are.

In 2016, I was teaching in Zimbabwe, and a young man shared his story of being called a failure by a girl he was dating, for not passing his exams. He shared how this had a negative impact on him, as she was telling people behind his back that he was stupid.

After this happened, the young man received encouragement from his parents who told him that he was a champion, that he was not stupid, and he could achieve whatever he set his mind to. This encouragement lifted his spirit and gave him the motivation he needed to be the best that he could be. He rejected the negative labels, worked hard, and passed the exams he'd failed initially.

Another example was shared by a young girl; let's call her Isabelle. When Isabelle was younger, she was told that she was lazy, rude, and too short. Isabelle explained that this hurt her feelings and that she felt inferior when she was around taller people. Isabelle even went on to say that she felt inferior at school and that she wouldn't be able to get good grades because she thought she was too short.

After some time, Isabelle realised that her height had nothing to do with her abilities. The day she took those labels off Isabelle became free, and she understood that despite what others had called her, she could do and become anything she wanted. Isabelle no longer lets the words of others hold her back. She's able to do this by challenging the negative words she hears.

From reading these examples, it is evident that the effects of being labelled are very significant. You may not realise, but people's words can either give you life—by increasing your self-esteem and pushing you towards your dreams and goals—or they can tear you down, thus breeding hurt, resentment, insecurity, and unhappiness.

Roger Crawford

Roger Crawford is a professional tennis player, a public speaker, and a best-selling author. Roger was born severely disabled, with a rare genetic defect—he has four impaired limbs. Yet, despite this, Roger is the only person in American history to have a severe disability and be a professional tennis association athlete and play a division 1 college sport.

Roger has been inducted into three different halls of fame (a hall of fame is a museum filled with plaques or busts honouring famous people), including the international speaker's hall of fame, and he has been recognised by *Sports Illustrated* to be "one of the most accomplished physically challenged athletes in the world."

Roger once said, *"We are a product of the choices we make, not the circumstances that we face."* Roger's life is inspiring because despite his **disability** he still chased his dream, despite being told that he would never be able to walk he chose not to let that deter him.

Roger's parents had told him *he was only as handicapped as he wanted to be.* This advice must have been life-changing for Roger, but I hope it is for you too!

I believe that these stories will inspire you not to give up on yourself despite what you've gone through. Keep going, try not to doubt yourself or base your abilities upon the expectations others have of you. You are not your past, and your past does not define who you are or who you will become.

Self-fulfilling prophecy

Self-fulfilling prophecy is similar to the labelling theory. However, the distinction between the two is that self-fulfilling prophecy is more behaviour related whereas labelling is speech related.

Self-fulfilling prophecy can be described as a prediction that becomes true either directly or indirectly. It entails positive or negative expectations regarding events, circumstances, or even people. Another definition states: *"Any positive or negative expectation about circumstances, events, or people that may affect a person's behaviour towards them in a manner that causes those expectations to be fulfilled."*

Here's an example of this definition in practice. In 1968, Robert Rosenthal a professor and Lenore Jacobson a primary school teacher conducted an experiment in an elementary school. The students undertook a test and teachers were told that certain students could expect to be "growth spurters" based upon the results of the Harvard Test of Inflected Acquisition. Unbeknown to the teachers, the test was not real and the students who were designated as "spurters" were randomly chosen. From conducting this experiment, Rosenthal and Jacobson expected to find changes in the student's achievements, based on the expectations their teachers had placed upon them.

The findings revealed that the expectations the teachers placed upon the students had significant effects on their performance. The students from whom teachers had high expectations obtained better grades.

This shows that teachers are more likely to say encouraging words and cheer on students who perform well and, in turn, the students on the receiving end continue to perform the way they are expected to, and become high achievers.

Regardless of the level the students were performing at, to begin with, more progress was made by those who received more praise and had higher expectations placed upon them. In essence, the teacher's verbalised expectations were a vital factor in determining the progress and achievements of the child.

The experiment is a good example of showing how people tend to behave in ways that are expected of them. In contrast, Oprah Winfrey's story illustrates that despite receiving negative labels, you can still take ownership of your life and make positive life choices (the ease of doing this varies according to the individual).

People like to label others and put them in boxes; however, nobody can control every aspect of a person's life. Some people have had a great head start while others may not be as privileged. This could be in terms of education, finances, separation of parents, growing up with an illness, growing up with one parent, or even not knowing who your biological parents are. Everyone has their own race to run and, regardless of the labels that society has placed upon you, it's important that you don't let others or your past define who you are or dictate who you become.

Knowing your value

When you know your value, it doesn't matter if the people around you don't recognise your worth. First, it's vital that you know your value even if you don't get affirmation from others.

Have you ever noticed that Rolls Royce and Bentley don't advertise as much as other companies?

Reason: They know that the value of their product brings customers to them.

Lesson: When you know your value, you don't have to beg people to like you, to be your friend, to spend time with you, or to love you.

Be confident in who you are. Not everyone can afford the luxury of your friendship.

— Unknown

My story

When I was growing up, I was rejected by close friends. I had a best friend who said, "I don't want to be your best friend anymore." Some close people that I was around didn't say nice things about me. I had friends who betrayed my trust, which resulted in the breakdown of some of my friendships.

As I got older, this affected me and I found it hard to trust people. Eventually, I put a wall around myself because I did not want others to get too close to me in case I got hurt again.

I used to ask myself—what's wrong with me? Why am I constantly **rejected**? Why am I constantly being hurt?

I felt people were treating me like I was *worthless*. Based upon how I felt, I believed those feelings and I took upon those labels. I started to believe that, when I talked, what I had to say was unimportant and not worth listening to.

As a direct result, my self-esteem decreased. (Remember, labels are not always given. Sometimes we feel we are something and associate ourselves with that thing, and actually label ourselves).

From my past experiences, I learned that *I* had put the label of rejection on me! I was wearing the label boldly across my head. I started to believe that I would always be rejected and—guess what? I started to see a pattern of rejection in my life! I noticed that when I was getting close to someone, I would purposely jeopardise the friendship so that they would pull away from me in case they hurt me.

Allow me to tell you about the day I took those labels off.

I went through those labels that had been placed upon me and I addressed them one by one. I sought to find out how they became labels and addressed my thoughts and feelings. I also put myself in my so-called friend's shoes and sought to make sense of their behaviour. Maybe they wanted to fit in? It could be that they didn't know any better?

However, regardless of the reason, I chose to forgive those that hurt me. This allowed me to move on and find closure, as I tended to ruminate about my past quite often.

I've been on a journey, and I'm now able to say I am a whole person today because I've rejected the negative labels and words placed upon me.

It's important that when people criticise us and try to hurt us, we don't take on board what they say and wear the labels they've given to us!

Rejecting what a person says can keep you free from hurt and free from the opinions of others. It's not always easy to do this especially when you hear those words repeatedly.

So, what you can do is challenge what was said, and ask yourself this question: "Is what this person saying true about me or is this just their opinion"?

People like to talk, and often too much! If you come across a person, who has nothing positive to say, remove or distance yourself from them. Why? Because it's not healthy to be around negative people as we become like the people, we surround ourselves with. Also, it can affect your self-esteem and the way you feel about yourself.

Exercise

What labels do you need to take off?
List the labels that you are wearing that have affected you.

- ____
- ____
- ____
- ____
- ____

What next?

Now you have completed your list. Draw a line through the negative labels and write down positive words about yourself.

It is time to move forward and leave the past behind. Decide today to forgive the people who have placed negative labels on you. This will help you to move forward and free you from negative emotions and feelings.

It's time for you to shift your attention from what others said you will become to looking towards the future. Focus on becoming the type of person you aspire to become.

What new labels will you put on?

If you like, find a person who you can do this exercise with and ask them to speak positive words about you.

Write down below the positive words with which you can identify.

- ______________________________

  ____

- ______________________________

  ____

- ______________________________

  ____

- ______________________________

  ____

- ______________________________

  ____

Now that you have done this exercise, how do you feel?

Identifying with these positive labels will enable you to move from what you identified yourself with, to how you see yourself now and also how you would like to be.

Regularly speaking positive words into your life will enable you to view yourself more positively. We are less likely to limit ourselves and our abilities when we see ourselves in a better light.

Chapter Summary

- Take off the negative labels that others have given you.
- You are not your past, neither does your past define who you are.
- Be confident in who you are because you are of great worth.
- We are a product of the choices we make, not the circumstances that we face.
- Be mindful of the company you keep and the type of people you are around—so-called friends can bring you down instead of uplifting you.

Summarise the key points you found in this chapter

Key 🗝

Key 🗝

Key 🗝

Key 🗝

Key 🗝

People are going to label you. It's how you overcome those labels that counts.

— One Tree Hill

CHAPTER 4

Confidence & Self-Esteem

Learn to love yourself for who you are

The topic of self-esteem is essential, as it can affect the choices one makes daily and can have significant implications as to how an individual turns out to be in their adult life.

Dove's 2014 self-esteem campaign revealed that seven in ten girls viewed themselves as not being good enough, or did not think that they measured up to society's standards (this was concerning their appearance, education, and their relationships with family and friends).

Furthermore, compared to 25 per cent of girls who had high self-esteem, 75 per cent of girls who had low self-esteem had been engaging in destructive and harmful activities and behaviours such as self-harming, disordered eating, bullying, smoking, and drinking.

The results show that destructive behaviour patterns are likely to be high among girls who have low self-esteem and poor body image, compared to those with high self-esteem. The results are heartbreaking, as they reveal that a high number of girls are not confident in who they are. And as a result, they may take part in destructive behaviour as a cry for help and as a means of coping.

Body image is the mental representation that one creates of oneself. It refers to an individual's feelings, thoughts, and perceptions that they have about their body, and plays a significant role in how one views oneself. The media is full of airbrushed perfected faces and bodies and many young males and females aspire to have the "ideal body"—a perfected look that is increasingly sought after. Body image also plays a significant role in one's self-esteem.

Self-esteem is something that can be built over time and can be linked with one's environment and upbringing. For example, being brought up in a loving environment where a person receives a lot of praise and admiration can boost self-esteem. Alternatively, being brought up in a controlling and belittling environment can result in low self-esteem.

In this chapter, we will explore how you view yourself, and the areas it can affect.

How do you see yourself?

As individuals, we tend to act in ways that are consistent with our internal images. Self-concept can be defined as the beliefs that one holds of oneself. Our self-concept is formed from the internal pictures and words we have of ourselves at any moment in time. These images of ourselves include beliefs, attitudes, abilities, and physical characteristics.

If a person views themselves as unlovable, unworthy, and a failure, their actions are likely to reflect their self-concept. To have a healthy self-concept and make positive progress in life, the way you view yourself has to be positive also.

Let's take a look at self-esteem, and how this can either push a person to excel or prevent them from progressing.

Self-esteem can be described as the confidence that a person has in their abilities, their value, and how they judge and evaluate themselves. The synonyms used for self-esteem are self-regard, faith in oneself, self-assurance, self-confidence and a sense of self-worth. In essence, self-esteem is how one sees oneself, and this can either be in a positive or negative light.

What does it mean to have high or low self-esteem?

A person who has a healthy opinion of themselves is confident in who they are, their abilities, and their value. Regardless of how they perform—well or poorly—they are able to adapt and move forward. A person with low self-esteem may not see their value and may think that they have little to offer.

A person who has low self-esteem is likely to view themselves as unworthy, inadequate, and even incapable. Low self-esteem is a thinking disorder that stems from having negative thinking patterns (also known as faulty thinking patterns), which involve irrational ways of thinking that do not represent the truth.

It can lead to problematic emotional states and behaviours, such as depression, anxiety, and conflicts in relationships. These negative patterns that are formed can permeate a person's every thought, to the point where ongoing self-defeating behaviour (self-sabotaging) occurs.

Here are some examples of negative thinking patterns

Filtering

Disregarding all the positive aspects of a situation as if they never happened and taking the negative details of a situation and magnifying them.

Black and white thinking

Also known as "all or nothing" thinking. This is the inability to see both the negative and positive aspects of our thoughts (there's no middle ground—it's one or the other).

Personalisation

The idea that the behaviours and actions of others are directed towards us. Blaming yourself for something that may not be entirely your fault. Alternatively, blaming others for our pain.

Overgeneralisation

Forming our conclusions based on a single event and generalising them to all our experiences/future experiences.

Labelling

Assigning unhealthy labels to ourselves or others—"I'm so clumsy." "They're so dumb."

Magnification/Minimisation

Making things bigger than they actually are or making something small so it seems less important.

Emotional reasoning

Automatically believing that what you feel about yourself must be true; for example, if you *feel* that you are uninteresting and stupid, then you must be.

Jumping to conclusions

Assuming that we know what others are thinking, and predicting what we think will happen based upon our assumptions (mind reading/fortune telling).

Disqualifying the positive

Disregarding the good things you've done or that have happened.

There are quite a few aren't there? I have saved one faulty thinking pattern so we can look at it in more detail. It's called Rumination (we all do this to an extent, some more than others).

Rumination

Rumination is a thought process that involves an individual repeatedly going over a thought. It consists of obsessive thinking that dwells upon thoughts and experiences. Rumination by itself isn't harmful as we all ruminate about situations and certain experiences. For example, constantly replaying an argument with a friend, dwelling upon difficulties or replaying past mistakes in your mind. However, it can become harmful and distressing when it involves negativity, anxiety and social anxiety. Rumination, therefore, can become an incorrect thinking pattern that can mould itself into how one thinks and become their norm.

It's crazy how our thoughts can dominate our lives, isn't it! **Our thoughts are so powerful that they have the ability to affect or behaviour and actions.**

Once you have a dominant, negative, reoccurring thought in your mind, it can be hard to let go of people and things that are associated with it. It's like your mind becomes infected, and you are now obsessed. You want to stop thinking about the mistake you made or what that person said, but it's hard to do so.

Thoughts come and go into our minds every day, without warning. The act of ruminating allows for certain negative thoughts and situations to stay in our mind for far too long.

Over time, what was once a thought becomes a seed and takes root—and roots are not always easy to dig out.

Not long after a seed has been planted, a shoot can often be seen. **Whatever thoughts you feed will grow** and will make themselves evident in your life, as our actions follow our thoughts.

Has a destructive thought ever come into your mind, and you questioned how it got there? "It isn't at all like me to be thinking like this"? Things can come into our minds that are not usually in line with how we tend to think, so be vigilant and protect your mind by monitoring what you allow in.

These examples show just how one's esteem can be affected, especially if a person has some of these negative thought patterns. It's essential, therefore, to challenge your thoughts and to think more positively about your situations and yourself.

Are you struggling with negative or destructive thoughts that you would like to eliminate from your mind?

Try this

1. Replace negative thoughts with positive thinking and affirmations. Consistency is key; the more you train your mind and choose to not dwell on negative unwanted thoughts the easier it will become.

2. If you find that you do need help with your thinking patterns, may I suggest seeking a therapist? They are very knowledgeable and can, in a practical way, help you deal with these distortions in depth. Your thinking patterns may be trauma-related.

Exercise

The way you view yourself is more important than how others see you

What is your self-perception? How did you come to believe this?

1. ______________________________

____

2. ______________________________

____

3. ______________________________

____

By doing this exercise, you're growing in awareness of how you perceive yourself. It will also enable you to identify why you see yourself the way you do and whether it stems from having positive or negative seeds sown into your life. For example, you may have received a lot of praise while growing up, or you may have been spoken down to, often as a child.

To view yourself in a better light, you need to change how you think. This process can take time but it's definitely possible. It's important that you think more positively.

Try to avoid meditating upon negative thoughts that enter your mind. By doing this those thoughts are less likely to take root in your thought life.

Second, in combination with this, it's important to question your negative thoughts. For example, a person who fails an exam may think that they're a "failure," and therefore incapable of passing **(Emotional reasoning)**.

However, by questioning their negative thoughts, they can try to rationalise the situation and view it from a different perspective: "Maybe I'm smarter than I think, I just need to revise a little longer for the next exam."

Is your self-esteem based upon how others perceive you?

It's not always the case but sometimes we think we're the problem. *"Oh* he's the second guy that's rejected me, there must be something wrong with me." "*They* keep giving me dirty looks." "They keep mocking the way I speak, I'm just not cool enough to fit in with that crowd." Hello! Just because people don't accept you, it doesn't mean something is wrong with you! It doesn't mean you're not good enough! It doesn't mean you have no value, and it certainly doesn't mean that you have little to offer. It's sad that our self-worth and self-esteem are so often linked to the opinions of others and the validation that we receive from them.

Think—they may have rejected you because they felt inferior to you, and wanted someone to dominate.

It may be that you're receiving dirty looks out of jealousy. They may mock your voice because they wished they spoke like you.

We often think the worst of ourselves when we don't understand the actions of others. But people often mistreat others due to their own insecurities and usually mirror how people have treated them in the past. This is dysfunctional behaviour on *their* part.

That being said, if you find yourself in a similar situation try not to let people's opinions or actions change your mood. **I've come to a place where I consciously choose not to let this affect me.**

This can be tricky to do at first, but the more you do it, the more natural it will become. Instead of saying "What's wrong with me?" I say to myself, "Maybe they're having a bad day." I don't see myself as the problem, and I go about my day in a carefree way.

When people do things that I don't quite understand, I try not to take it personally. A lot of the times we think we're at fault or that something is wrong with us. Statements like, "Did I do something wrong?" and "I'm just not good enough" used to run through my mind when I had unwanted encounters with people. Then, one day, I started to question those negative thoughts and realised those thoughts were not actually valid.

You are unique in your own right, and not everyone will see that. Try not to let the opinions of others define how you view yourself. *"Your value doesn't decrease based on someone's inability to see your worth."* — Unknown

Dealing with offence

A lot of times we take offence too quickly, and as a result, we harbour hurt and bitterness. For example, you say hello to someone and they ignore and walk straight past you, loads of thoughts may come rushing to your mind. "They purposely ignored me, what did I do?" or "They are so fake, one minute they are saying hi, the next minute they can't see me"?

Instead of being negative about the matter, try to be a bit more carefree and see the situation from a different perspective—"Maybe they didn't hear me."

Reacting this way does not erase what happened, but it keeps you more in control of your emotions and the situation, allowing you to think more clearly and preventing spite from building up.

In summary, it's important to acknowledge how we feel as we are all human and all have emotions. However, it's also important not to harbour negative thoughts and to quickly move on. Why? Because taking offence can be time-consuming and may not allow us to progress with that person or with that situation.

Whatever you focus on will magnify

If you focus on positive things more than the negative, you're likely to be a more positive person and have more positive thoughts and a positive attitude towards life. Similarly, if you focus on negative things (e.g., what you don't like about yourself), you're only going to feel worse than you already do and you're less likely to accept yourself for who you are.

Starting from today, make it a habit to focus on the positives.

Why? Because focusing on the positives helps you to be less self-critical and to readily dismiss self-defeating thoughts. By doing this you will find that the more positive you are about yourself, the higher your self-esteem will become.

Focus on the positive

Exercise

Write down three things that YOU feel makes you unique

1. ____

2. ____

3. ____

If people were to describe you, what three positive words would they say?

1. ____

2. ____

3. ____

How did you find doing the exercise above?

When I have asked people previously to do the first part of this exercise, I learned that a lot of them found it difficult to recognise the good things they liked about themselves.

People tend to know the things they don't like about themselves instantly. They can even think of good things to say about others from the top of their heads, but not about themselves.

Why?

First, we tend to think about the negative more than the positive. Second, a lot of people don't know themselves. We all take time to get to know others, but do we take time to get to know ourselves?

Take some time to explore who you are as a person and ask yourself the following questions:

What are my likes and dislikes?

Why am I the way I am?

What's the thing that drives me to get up in the morning?

What are my standards?

What are my values?

What's important to me?

These exercises are stepping stones for you to learn more about yourself. They also are an excellent way for you to focus on the positive aspects of who you are, and will help you to appreciate yourself and the person you are becoming.

Focusing more on the positive aspects of yourself does not rule out working on the things you desire to change. Neither does it stop you from working on positive ways that you could adopt to improve aspects of yourself that you may not like. For example, you may be overweight and self-critical, but being more positive about yourself and your situation can help to improve your outlook in setting goals to achieve your ideal weight.

Whereas if you are self-critical and negative, your mind may not be focused on developing you as a person. You may not have a desire to develop goals and make positive improvements because of the negative thoughts you have of yourself.

Focusing on the positive more than the negative is likely to motivate you and drive you forward.

Now there have been times when I have set targets and goals for myself, for example, something as simple as getting out of bed on time so that I have enough time to get ready.

If I was going somewhere and I was running late, I would usually beat myself up "Why didn't you get up on time?" "You always do this."

In situations like this, I got angry at myself and I don't like being mad at myself, because I like me!

So, I try and be positive. Even though I'm not happy, I don't call myself names. In the past, I would say "You're always late" and I would see a pattern of lateness—I reaped what I sowed. So, I would tell myself "Next time, I'll be on time," and I would make a plan: "Go to bed earlier, limit time on social media, iron your clothes from the night before, and so on." Sometimes, for you to make a change, you have to be tired of having to go through the same thing, but you can still be positive in doing so. **Being positive is progressive, as it puts your mind in the right frame to make changes.**

Freedom from self-comparison

When I was freed from my past, I realised my worth, and I stopped comparing myself to all the other girls around me. There will always be someone who has what you may desire: longer hair, perfect teeth, and so on.

When I was around twenty-three years of age, I became more secure in myself and in who I was. I realised that if I kept comparing myself to everybody else around me, I'd never be happy with who I truly am because I'd always be looking at my flaws and what I don't have instead of noticing how amazing I am.

In today's society, there's a lot of pressure for girls to look a certain way (and it is common for boys not to show their vulnerability and, if they do, they aren't seen to be masculine). I've learned the importance of trying not to live up to other people's expectations because they're not living my life; they're not going through what I'm going through, so why should their thoughts and opinions dictate my life?

I don't need a compliment from anyone saying that I look good, or a "well done" for doing something; of course, compliments are nice and encouragement and appreciation are even better, but I don't need them to feel a sense of worth. My worth isn't in the compliments or even the recognition that I receive; I already know that I'm one of a kind.

You were born to stand out, stop trying to fit in!

You are unique and set apart

That being said, I want to encourage you to love yourself. A lot of us look at the lives of those around us and wish we had what they have.

Look less at what the media calls "beautiful" and start accepting yourself for who you are.

We compare ourselves to society and worry whether we fit in, but: guess what? You were made to stand out; you were made to be different. You are unique.

Magazines tell us what looks good, what the latest trends are, how we can be less of that (and more of this), and we can find ourselves continually trying to keep up. It doesn't end. What's sad is that so many people are suffering. People are depressed and insecure because they are always comparing themselves to a standard that's fake.

The birthmark on your neck represents you coming into the world! Those freckles on your face make you unique. That scar on your hand has its own story. We hide our imperfections, yet it is our imperfections that make us unique and stand out.

Why is it that we try to hide our imperfections?

We hide them because we feel vulnerable, we feel like society won't accept us, or would be disgusted by them.

But everyone is struggling with their battles and insecurities, and hiding how we feel doesn't make things better. It just makes us more closed and inaccessible. When we share our insecurities and vulnerabilities with others, it makes us more relatable, and people don't feel like they are alone in their problems. Better yet, it allows us to open up, which can help us to feel less pressured and burdened.

The "media" often sells us false information. The models we see only look the way they do because Photoshop enhanced their looks. People scroll through Instagram, read magazines, and can be saddened because they start to compare themselves, wishing they had what others had. The lifestyle that people post online is not necessarily the one they are living. We live in a "want to be perfect society" yet so many people don't have their lives "together". How do we know if the person behind the picture is happy and secure in themselves? They may be unhappy and searching for change.

People only put the best parts of their lives up on social media but, these are just highlights of their life. Behind every trailer is a movie, behind every movie is a reality! Everyone has their own experiences, and we should never judge a book by its cover.

The "media" alone is not to blame for this self-comparing society that we live in. Some of the negative views people have about themselves can sit closer to home. For example, people are constantly emotionally abused by family members, close friends, and their partners. This alone can have damaging effects on one's self- worth and how they view themselves in comparison to others.

How many people have you seen who had it all going for them yet, all of a sudden, to your surprise they suffered a mental breakdown, fell into depression, or committed suicide? Think for a minute. Not everyone speaks up about what they are going through and how they are feeling. Is it possible that when people face these challenging times and feel like it's never-ending; they may fall into depression and could become suicidal, thinking they're alone. And at times even believe the lie that the world would be a better place without them?

With the advancement of technology, the society we live in has connected yet has isolated so many individuals. Are we using social media for its intended purposes which is to connect with people or do we find ourselves comparing our lives with each other instead? It's important that we stop and speak to people, ask someone how their day is going and be genuine in your response. I've asked this question many times to find a range of different answers. Sometimes people want to talk, but they may not want to initiate a conversation. It could be that someone's going through a tough period and may benefit from some support. That being said, make an effort to reach out to those around you, you may feel a sense of connectedness by doing this and hopefully spend less time comparing yourself with others because you're connecting with them.

Depression

Depression is prevalent and affects over ten thousand young people in England alone. According to the World Health Organization, (2019), depression is a common mental health disorder, affecting over 300 million people of all ages worldwide. It is a result of various interactions of biological, psychological, and social factors. Young people are facing various pressures, including bullying, stress at school, body image issues, and pressure from social media. As a result, some have found themselves in depressive states.

If you are going through depression or suffer from anxiety or have a matter that is troubling you, please note that there is always help available. Seek help from those around you, as there are people who care for you, even if you don't feel like there are. Request counselling and support, as there will always be someone you can talk to. There are also various interventions and programs that can help improve and correct depressive symptoms.

Practical steps on how to build your self-esteem

Have daily affirmations- Speak and concentrate on the positive aspects of yourself (Create your own list of affirmations).

I am special
I am unique
I am loveable
I know my worth

Think of positive things that you can say about yourself, write them down, and stick them around your room.

Become accustomed to building yourself up. As you build yourself up daily, the negative views you have will decrease (Try to avoid negative self-talk such as criticising yourself).

Spend time with people who will actively uplift you.

This should help in building your confidence (Surround yourself with people who are confident—their confidence may rub off on you).

Question your negative thoughts, examine how they got there, and replace them with positive ones.

Watch motivational videos that are uplifting and empowering.

Learn a new skill.

Push yourself out of your comfort zone.

Learn to embrace who you are, paying attention to what you like about yourself.

There is a purpose for your life. However, if you place more effort and attention on the things that you're not happy with, your focus will not be in the right place, and you won't be as effective in becoming the person you could become.

There is nothing wrong in making changes with things you're not happy with, but it can become a problem if you're solely focusing on what you don't like and thinking negatively. Try to find a solution.

For example, you may be unhappy with your fitness level. But instead of taking actions to improve your fitness, you moan to your friends about how out of shape you are. The problem arises when you stay in this realm. Your mindset should be focused on improving negative circumstances rather than wallowing in them.

Exercise

What ways do you compare yourself to others?

1. ____

2. ____

3. ____

How does comparing yourself to others make you feel about your self-perception?

Does it help to raise your self-esteem or lower it? Why?

Self-acceptance

Self-acceptance is the ability to embrace good strengths and not-so-positive strengths. It is unconditional and comes without judgment. An individual who accepts who they are doesn't judge their self-worth by their performance or what others think of them. It also means not needing everyone to like you to feel worthy. It starts with the opinion you have of yourself.

The humanistic stance of psychology holds that self-acceptance is a journey of self-discovery.

From my experience, and of those around me, I have found this to be true. As we get older, we tend to be more content and accepting of who we are because we know ourselves better and have gained more confidence.

When you accept yourself for who you are, without harsh judgment, your possibilities can become limitless.

Why is this? Ultimately, you're no longer holding yourself back. A person who has high levels of self-acceptance is likely to have a positive approach towards the things they face in life.

A person who accepts themselves for who they are knows that they're not perfect, but doesn't need to compare themselves to others because they are happy with who they are.

A person who scores high on self-acceptance does not wish to be any different than they currently are.

Wow, this is a fantastic place to be!

In a nutshell, self-acceptance is about allowing yourself to grow, remembering that you are not a finished article and are a work in progress.

Chapter Summary

- Try not to take things too personally.
- Stop trying to fit in and impress people. Express yourself and be who you are.
- Stop comparing yourself to others.
- When you accept who you are, there's less room for comparison.
- Build yourself up daily by speaking words of encouragement into your life.
- You are unique and more significant than you realise.
- Always remember that you are beautiful, and are one of a kind. There is so much greatness within you yet to be birthed!
- We have to be our own fans, and rejoice in who we are.
- Try to stop doubting yourself and your abilities; stop seeing yourself as the problem. Then you will give yourself the opportunity to be free and to believe in who you are.

Summarise the key points you found in this chapter

Key 🗝

Key 🗝

Key 🗝

Key 🗝

Key 🗝

What you think about yourself is much more important than what people think of you.

— Seneca

CHAPTER 5

Character

What Kind of Person are You?

A person who wants nothing, never can be bought

A person who won't fight, never can be fought

A person who doesn't lie, never can be caught

A person who won't play the game, never can be used

A person who doesn't cheat, will always pay his dues

A person who never thinks, can never have any views

A person who doesn't care what you think, will never leave you confused

A person who has nothing, they will never lose

Tell me dear friend, what kind of person are you?

— Pauline Russell

Becoming a person of character

In this chapter, we will be exploring what it means to be a person of character, it's importance, and why it's something that you should continually try to develop.

Character can be defined as:

- "The aggregate of features and traits that form the individual nature of some person or thing."

- "The particular combination of qualities in a person or place that makes them different from others."

In the Bible, a man called Paul rejoiced in his hardships; he said: "We rejoice in our sufferings, knowing that suffering produces endurance, and endurance produces character" (Rom. 5:3–5).

Paul ultimately is saying that the suffering he went through helped in the development of his character. Endurance produces character!

Endurance in its simplest form is to see something through, despite adverse conditions. Throughout this book, it is evident that whatever you go through, whether it's something you're trying to overcome or whether it's taking active steps to improve your abilities, the process is what produces character. Our experiences humble us; they make us wiser, and they make us more compassionate as well as stronger individuals. Our experiences not only teaches us but also shapes and moulds us into who we are becoming.

Without going through a process, how can a person be built? It's the lessons of a person's journey that helps to develop their character.

Have you ever heard of the phrase, "That's a person of character."? Well, it's often associated with a person who has a good character.

A person associated with having good character can be described as honest, reliable, courageous, and integral. A person of good character can be relied upon because they tend to stick to their word and do what they say, they are consistent with their actions, and this is known by those around them. Furthermore, a person with good character is known to have integrity and is honest and truthful even when nobody is around to see.

Here are a few definitions of Integrity:

- "The state of being whole and undivided."
- "The quality of being honest and having strong moral principles."

In simple terms, integrity means to be at one with oneself. Therefore, a person who is at one with themselves will say something and act according to what they say. Their words and actions are in sync. On the other hand, a person known for having little character will say one thing but do something different; their actions are out of line with their words. They tend to be divided against themselves, and you won't always know what to expect from them. They may say they will do something, but if they don't feel like it, it may not get done.

Why is character so important?

A person of integrity can be trusted by those around them, so character is important because it's what builds trust. It's difficult to look up to someone you don't trust. When it comes to leadership and responsibility in work situations, for example, employers want people who they can trust and rely on. Am I right in thinking that if you had your own company, you would want someone of good character to work for you?

Myles Munroe once said, "Lead with your life, your life is the weight of your words." In essence, where you are today is a result of doing what you said. People may listen to what you say, but they watch what you do even more closely; by this, they know whether you can actually follow through with your words. Many people advise others, yet they can't take their own advice. I guess the best thing you can do is to let your actions do the talking.

I want to encourage you to desire to become a person of character. Why? Because you will live a more effective life, you'll accomplish what you set out to achieve. People around you are also likely to look up to you because you won't compromise your values as you know who you are and you do what you say.

Becoming a person of character is a process, and, within that process, you can decide who you want to become.

Exercise

List five good character traits that you have, along with the actions you have taken to be this way. For example:

Trait: I have integrity

Action: I am a person of integrity because I am faithful to the standards I have and my beliefs. I don't compromise despite the opinions of others and what they say.

Trait: ______________________________

Action: ______________________________

____

Trait: ______________________________

Action: ______________________________

____

Trait: ______________________________

Action: ______________________________

____

Trait: ______________________________

Action: ______________________________

____

Trait: ______________________________

Action: ______________________________

____

Now, in detail, list five traits that you would like to change
For example:

Trait: Become less stubborn and be more accepting of people's views.

Action: Listen to others more; allow them to express their opinions without disregarding what they have to say.

Trait: ______________________________

Action: ______________________________

____

Trait: ______________________________

Action: ______________________________

____

Trait: ______________________________

Action: ______________________________

____

Trait: ______________________________

Action: ______________________________

____

Trait: ______________________________

Action: ______________________________

____

Notice, above, how I said "To be less stubborn"; no one is perfect, but we can strive to become better. So, by saying less it indicates that I acknowledge that I am a work in progress, but I am still actively working on ways that I can improve.

For you to see desired results, this exercise requires you to be self-reflective of your actions and being consistent in implementing desired behaviours.

Why is this exercise important?

- It helps you to build character and to better yourself.
- People around you will notice the difference in you, and you can even suggest this exercise for them to do. Why not start a character challenge where those around you join in? That way you can monitor each other's progress.
- You're also likely to be respected more by others around you *"Knowledge will give you power, but character respect"* — Bruce Lee.

This exercise demonstrates that by taking small steps, you have the ability to create the desired changes you wish to see in your life.

People with good intentions make promises.
People with good character keep them.

— Unknown

Can you rely on yourself?

Have you ever heard of the phrase "Let your yes be your yes and your no be your no"? Well, my interpretation of this is not to beat around the bush. If you say you're going to do something, commit yourself to do it; if you offer to help someone out, do it. Be true to your word. Why is this? You see, when you say you're going to do something and you don't do it, you become less reliable to yourself but also to others. Disclaimer—sometimes we do commit to things we shouldn't commit to, and realise this later, but I am talking in general terms.

So, ask yourself, how do I feel when I don't do what I've set out to do? Does that feeling result in action towards completing your goal or does it hinder you, and make you feel worse about yourself and slow you down? Our feelings often operate whether we do things or not; oftentimes when we don't feel like doing something, we don't do it. Why? Because we may not feel like it; there may be no motivation to do what we have set out to do, or there are no severe consequences for our lack of action.

We tend to do the things we don't want to do usually when money is attached to it, or an outcome that we don't desire will occur without our action. For example, your parents have asked you to help tidy the house; now, in most instances for you, there is no rush to tidy up—who likes cleaning, right? But you know if you don't do it, there are consequences, and it is the fear of these consequences that usually motivates people in general to do things. This isn't a good form of motivation but, it somehow gets the job done. Sometimes fear can be a good motivating force in getting things done.

Finish what you start

Have you found there have been times where you can't fully trust yourself to do the things that you have committed to or want to do? You see, the more times you set out to do a task, and you fail to do it, your self-trust decreases; in turn, this can decrease the confidence that you have in yourself and your abilities. I found that if I set out to do something but ended up doing something else, I would feel like I let myself down because I wasn't achieving what I know I set out to do.

When I set my mind to do a task and accomplished it, I would feel a sense of achievement, and this would make me happy because I achieved my desired results. Having these desirable results would push and spur me on to keep pursuing my goals. The lesson in this is that we become more confident in ourselves and with our abilities when we prove to ourselves that we can be consistent in achieving what we set out to do.

In life, there may be things that you don't want to do, but for desired results to occur, they have to be done. I was not too fond of taking exams in school but I had to take them in order to pass. I would not say I liked doing essays at university, but they had to be done. There were even a few times when I stayed over at university without getting any sleep. Those times were tough: I was drained; I was tired. At times, I felt like putting work off until another time, but I knew the results I wanted, and that motivated me to keep going. My experiences disciplined me and taught me the importance of dedication.

To be productive, with my time and work, I also learned that I worked best with regimes and timetables. In my case, the lesson was that I needed consistency, order, and routine. As a result, I found that I was able to follow through with the things I started, my life became more structured, and I found having a routine helped me to be more productive. **I achieved more things!**

In some cases, the lesson could be character related—you may need to go through some experiences to make you humble or to make you less self-consumed.

Take a look at the sport boxing—boxers have to stick to a strict diet and a rigorous fitness routine, which is very intense and requires discipline, dedication, and hard work. Possessing discipline and dedication are not necessarily what makes a person win a fight, but they are required for a person to be suitable to fight. It's certainly not easy, and it isn't all fun and games, but it is necessary for growth and progress. The people that do this may not want to get up early to train in the morning, but it has to be done if they're going to see their desired results. The reality is, it's not about how you feel.

To be successful, you must be willing to do the things today others won't do in order to have the things tomorrow others won't have.

— Les Brown

Look at P. Diddy. He is known as an entrepreneur, Grammy award-winning record producer, artist, songwriter, screenwriter, and philanthropist. However, he's not where he is today by chance, or based on how he felt; all of the things he has achieved are down to his consistent work ethic. One of P. Diddy's mottoes is "Sleep is for losers" okay, that's a bit crazy, because I love to sleep, but I get the point behind his statement. He has a drive for success that keeps him awake. To have all these accomplishments under his belt, P. Diddy must have had a serious mind-set. He was serious about his dreams but he was also a realist. He was aware of what he had to do to become successful and the man that he is today. Get used to being uncomfortable when those around you are having fun and are going out, work on your dream, you can't be average if you want to go far in life. P. Diddy said that "There is a time and a place for everything." Basically have fun, live life, but know that for greatness to be birthed, sacrifices need be made.

Michael Jackson had a passion for music, but his love for it did not just get him the title king of pop by chance. As a child, he and his brothers were extremely disciplined and had a strict regime, and Michael kept this up even in his solo career. It was his work ethic and the sacrifices that he made while growing up—for instance, having a particular diet, maintaining a specific image, regular vocal lessons, and choreography practice day after day, which enabled his greatness to be birthed.

Michael Jackson most likely had mornings when all he wanted to do was lie in, maybe even take a break and live a normal childhood. But music was Michael Jackson's motivation, and this pushed him, even when times were difficult.

In an interview with Oprah Winfrey, Michael Jackson said, "It is just so much work, people are used to just seeing the outcome, but they never get to see the side of the work you go through to produce that outcome." Other than singing, Michael Jackson was known and is famous for various other things—he was a philanthropist, a humanitarian, an actor, a dancer, a songwriter, the list goes on. In his short life, he achieved so much for just one man, and his life goes to show a lot can be achieved, especially when hard work, consistency, and passion are involved.

Find your motivation

What's your motivation behind the things you do?

I was motivated to do my degree for a few reasons—firstly, because I wanted to better myself. However, I questioned my abilities and whether I was even smart enough to do the degree that I wanted to study. Secondly, after initial resistance, I decided to go to the university upon receiving encouragement from people who believed in me. They told me that I have what it takes and that I can do anything that I put my mind to. This helped me to believe in myself and my abilities despite how I initially felt.

Thirdly, I decided to do my degree so that I could learn and acquire new skills and pass on knowledge. And this will enable me to help and encourage young people in my community and around the world to make the best of their lives despite the odds they may feel are against them.

I'll take character over reputation. Your character is what you really are, while your reputation is merely what others think of you.

— A. J. Perez

Your company and your character

Do not be deceived: "*Bad company ruins good morals*" (1 Corinth. 15:33).

Have you ever heard the saying "show me a person's friends and I can tell you where they are heading"? Or, "show me your friends and I'll tell you who you are." Well, it's evident that we become like those we are around, therefore your company can affect your character!

Jim Rohn said, "You are the average of the five people you spend the most time with." Interesting statement. This raises the question of whether I am around the right kind of people? This is an important, yet a difficult question, because you would not be around someone you do not like (well, in most cases). A lot of the people we call friends have at some point in our lives been there for us through our difficulties, have given advice, and have been a shoulder to lean on. There comes a point where among these friends you have to separate the good influencers from the bad.

How do the people around you treat you? Are they respectful to your thoughts and opinions? Do they listen to what you have to say? Are they reliable? Do they belittle you? Do they make frequent snide comments about you? Do they embarrass you frequently? Are they really your friends? Do they only check in on you when they want something?

The reason I'm asking these questions is because it's important that you have friends who are genuinely your friends but also are of good character, Why? So that you can rely on them. And they will more than likely be trustworthy.

We all want friends who can push and motivate us. This is important, however, make sure these friends are also going in the right direction. You can have a person around you helping you, but are they going in your direction and are they doing the right things.

For example, if you're around people who are negative, guess what, you are likely to be negative, too. What is the mind-set and mentality of those around you like? If the people that you are around are not showing you a better way to live your life, aren't supporting or inspiring you to become better, then you may want to take a good look at your circle of influences. Assess whether they will be a help or hindrance to your life. Even my circle of friends now is smaller than it was last year.

Here are some further questions to ask yourself:

1. Are the people around me good or bad influences?
   Explain how? (You may need to break this one down to individual names.)

2. What direction in life am I heading in?

3. How can I be a better influence on those around me?

4. Are those around me supportive of my dreams and do they motivate me to do/become better?

These types of questions are significant because they should prompt you to think about who you are, and who your friends are. Furthermore, they should cause you to think about the type of person you wish to become and whether you can become that type of person with the people that are around you now. Are the people in your friendship circles at this moment going in the same direction as you? And do they encourage you to pursue your dreams and goals?

Chapter Summary

- A person of character has integrity and can be relied upon by those around them.
- Your actions shouldn't be based upon your feelings. Putting in hard work now produces good results later.
- Our character develops as we work on ourselves and achieve the outcomes we desire.
- A man of character needs friends of character. We become like the people we surround ourselves with, so be cautious/picky with the people that you allow to be around you.
- In life, to get to where you want to go, don't follow everyone. Choose wisely who you follow.

Summarise the key points you found in this chapter

Key 🗝

Key 🗝

Key 🗝

Key 🗝

Key 🗝

People of character do the right thing even if no one else does, not because they think it will change the world but because they refused to be changed by the world.

— Michael Josephson

CHAPTER 6

Legacy

Legacy can be described as:

- "Something that someone has achieved that continues to exist after they stop working or they die."
- "Something left or handed down by a predecessor."
- "The principle that a thing exists as a result of something that happened in the past can later be used in a different way."

Why is our legacy important?

Our legacy is not just about the money we leave behind (businesses, property, etc.) or even how well known we are. Our legacy is about the impact our lives have had on others and its ability to initiate progressive change. Therefore, how we live our lives is of great importance as it determines the influence we have upon others and the possibilities this can have in creating a better environment. We will naturally leave legacies, the question is, what kind of legacy do you want to leave?

Often, we may find ourselves thinking about the present, but it is also important to think about the future, because the way we live our lives today will affect our lives and the people around us tomorrow.

The People's Champion

Muhammed Ali was a man who had a large following and certainly left his mark on this earth. Ali was known as a professional boxer but was also known as a philanthropist and an activist—**a pillar in his community and a person who fought for change amongst his people.** Some would say *he* was the greatest boxer to have ever lived. Some title! —But what made him so great? Was it the fifty-six wins he had under his belt? Was it all his achievements throughout his boxing career? Or was there something more?

Dream disruption

Yes, Ali brought a new style to the sport—and yes, he won the heavy weight championship three times and was the first to do so (A heavy weight is a boxer who weighs more than 175 pounds, therefore, they are in the heaviest class. Whereas, a lightweight is a professional boxer who weighs between 130-135 pounds). But most especially, he won the hearts of many around the world.

Whilst studying Muhammed Ali, I discovered that during his professional career he was called to serve in the army—of which he refused to serve due to his religious beliefs against violence. This led to Muhammed Ali being suspended from boxing for three years. After reading his story, it dawned upon me, what seemed like a disruption to his professional career turned out to be a door that allowed him to play an active role in producing societal change. This caused him to not just be known as a professional boxer, but also as an activist and a philanthropist. Muhammed Ali stood up for racial equality. He stood for what he believed was his rights and the rights of others.

Ali's story is a great example, in showing that although we make plans, for example, what career path we want to go down, life doesn't always go to plan. However, changes to our plans can be beneficial to us and those around us.

The heavy weight

I could talk about Muhammed Ali and his achievements all day but I want to talk about a legacy which he left behind—his youngest daughter, Laila Ali. Children are a part of their parent's legacy. They are their parent's bloodline. The parents' influence lives through their children long after they die. Therefore, how we live our lives determines the impact we will have upon others. Laila Ali followed her father's footsteps to become a professional boxer. Laila mentions in an interview that despite her father being Muhammed Ali, she did not think to become a boxer until she saw a fight between two female boxers for the first time on TV. It's interesting that she followed her father's path of boxing indirectly!

Laila Ali is known as a former professional boxer, holding under her belt the title of being the four–time undefeated world champion. She is also known for being a fitness and wellness expert, the founder of the Laila-Ali lifestyle and a TV host. Laila's sphere of influence is large and she herself has created a great legacy.

Can you see how our sphere of influence can be handed down to the next generation?

Becoming and leaving a legacy

You can impact the world and leave a legacy by living a life that empowers those around you

Here's an example of the legacy I would like to leave.

I want to be a woman known for living a selfless life. A woman who served her community and various countries worldwide. A lover of people, travel, and life. One who encouraged and empowered others to step outside their comfort zone and become better. A woman full of passion.

What Kind of legacy do you want to leave?

Mother Teresa

"The saint of the gutters"

Mother Teresa was known for her selfless and extraordinary missionary work in India amongst the poor and the destitute. She was canonised by the catholic church in 2016 and was named Saint Teresa of Calcutta. She was classed as one of the greatest humanitarians who served in the twentieth century.

1928

At the age of eighteen, Mother Teresa decided to become a nun and moved to Calcutta. She worked at an all-girls school called St. Mary's and taught history and geography. She later became the head mistress teaching and helping the city's poorest Bengali families.

1946

Mother Teresa felt led by God to stop teaching and to dedicate her time to help those who were extremely poor and sick in the slums of Calcutta. During the period of the 1950s and 1960s, Mother Teresa founded several mobile health clinics—a family health clinic, a nursing home, a leper colony, and an orphanage.

1979

Mother Teresa was awarded a noble peace prize, which recognised her service in helping those suffering. Mother Teresa is the founder of the Order of the Missionaries Charity, which encompassed a group of Roman Catholic women/missionaries who dedicated their time serving the poor. Numerous centres were also opened which offered aid to the terminally ill, elderly and disabled just to name a few. Today, there are services under The Mother

Teresa Foundation that offer homes for the elderly free of charge, medical assistance, and scholarships within their educational programme.

There is so much more I could say about Mother Teresa and the lasting impact her life has had on this world. Her work and life inspire me, to be more, be my best, be selfless, and look out intentionally for others as well as those around me. She truly led a life full of service and empowered those around her to do the same. Mother Teresa's legacy lives on and many people across the world to this day are benefiting from the work that she and her companions did.

Now, you may not build an orphanage or even open a nursing home but I hope that Mother Teresa's legacy and the life she lived inspire you to live a life that seeks to help others.

What kind of person would you like to be remembered as?

Think-on how this will bring clarity for the type of person you are and what changes you could make to reach that ideal.

Now that you know how you would like to be remembered, let's go a little deeper.

Why do you want to be remembered this way? Knowing your why should encourage and push you to walk out your life effectively.

Steve changed the tech game forever!

When it comes to technology, there is no doubt that Steve Jobs is a genius! Known as an inventor and businessman and if you don't already know—Steve Jobs is one of the founders of Apple.

Adopted and a college dropout, Steve Jobs made the most of his life. Steve was known as a character for many different things, and though he was one of the founders of Apple he was forced to leave his own company due to disagreements with the CEO at the time. Once Steve left Apple he went on to start another computer company known as NeXT computers. However, though the computers were sophisticated, the computers failed to sell on a mass level and therefore the line wasn't so successful. Steve also brought Pixar and became the majority shareholder of Pixar and the chairman. Steve's stewardship helped the company create edge cutting successful high-profile films such as Toy Story, Finding Nemo, and The Incredibles.

Who doesn't have an iPhone?

This is where the story becomes interesting! In 1997, Apple brought NeXT which led to Steve returning to Apple where he acted as an interim CEO. Steve undeniably came at a crucial time for Apple as they were finding it difficult to make a profit. Now back at Apple, Steve's creative genius unleashed and he cut down on a number of their products, focusing only on four. Not long after Steve's return the company soared to great heights and in 2017, the iPhone sold 223 million units becoming the top-selling tech product that year. As of 2018, Apple was known as the first company in the US to be worth $1 trillion dollars.

Within Job's lifetime, he was able to transform six industries such as mobile phones, computers, animated movies, music, digital publishing, and tablet computing.

At the age of fifty-six, after battling with pancreatic cancer for many years, in 2011, Steve Jobs passed away. Though Steve is no longer here with us, his legacy still lives on. There are many books written about Steve Jobs such as *The Presentation Secrets of Steve Jobs*, *Steve Jobs: The Man Who Thought Different*, and *The Innovation Secrets of Steve Jobs*. It is clear that Steve was a genius and there is a lot that can be learned from him.

What interest me about Steve's story is that he was passionate about what he did and was consistent in working on his craft and delivering ideas and products. He learnt how to combine technological advancement with artistry, resulting in a technological revolution. Steve wasn't just an inventor or an entrepreneur but a pioneer.

Steve also taught me the importance of FOCUS, he cut out many of the products Apple was working on because he knew that focusing on a few things would receive greater time and attention—which resulted in quality products being produced. What are you focusing on right now? Is it important? Could you prioritise your attention more in certain areas so that you're more effective?

Using your talents and passions what difference do you want to make in the world?

____

____

____

____

____

____

After reading about these three amazing people, I hope that it has encouraged you to rise above your circumstances and to take ownership of your dreams and passions. Do not let life consume you—a lot of things may try to disrupt you from reaching your full potential but I want to encourage you to push through the disruptions, excel and achieve.

To make lasting changes in your life, it's imperative that you go the extra mile and attempt more than you're used to doing. When you study, go all out; when you train, train as hard as you can. In all that you do, put 110 per cent into it. If it's worth doing, give it your all and—most importantly—never give up.

Learn to become a person of excellence and the results will speak for themselves. I want to encourage you to try and become better than the person you were yesterday. I'm sure you've heard the term before "It's not about being better than everybody else but about becoming a better person". And you may be asking yourself how *do* I become a better person? That's a great question!

- Educate yourself by reading more.
- Learn and research the answers to your questions.
- Learn and develop new skills and devote time to practice your craft.
- Frequently go out of your comfort zone.
- Don't just settle in a job, relationship, business venture, or anything that does not inspire you to aim higher.
- Connect with those around you and intentionally make new friends. The phrase "it's not what you know but who you know" is very significant in terms of social mobility and being exposed to potentially life-changing opportunities and relationships.
- Be intentional about the type of person you wish to become.

Chapter Summary

- We leave a legacy through our service to others.
- Be intentional about the person you wish to become.
- Leaving a legacy isn't just about what one accomplishes during his or her lifetime and what they've left behind but more so how they enable those around them.
- Focus your attention—the three people mentioned above were all focused on what they were doing.
- Don't become so entangled in the present that you pay the future no attention.
- Your legacy starts with you.

Summarise the key points you found in this chapter

Key 🗝

Key 🗝

Key 🗝

Key 🗝

Key 🗝

Without leaps of imagination, or dreaming, we lose the excitement of possibilities. Dreaming, after all, is a form of planning.

— Gloria Steinem

Dear Reader, this is the end of the book but the beginning of a new journey. It's time to Arise and Shine!

Notes

Chapter 1

Arise & Shine

https://www.virgin.com/travel/why-did-richard-branson-start-airline

Schill, Nancy. (2014). *Coach-in-Box—Goal setting workbook: Target and achieve your goals at work*. Austin, TX: ExecIntel Solutions, LLC.

Ndu, U. I. (2018). *Set smart goals and accomplish them: Practical goal setting guide and workbook*. Springlight Books.

http://ksoo.com/a-best-selling-author-overcomes-multiple-disabilities/

http://www.espn.com/sportscentury/features/00016048.html

http://www.newsweek.com/missing-cut-382954

Chapter 2

Purpose & Passion

Conzemius, A., & O'Neill, J. (2009). *The power of SMART goals: Using goals to improve student learning*. Bloomington, IN: Solution Tree Press.

https://www.huffingtonpost.com/marymorrissey/the-power-of-writing-down_b_12002348.html

https://www.biographyonline.net/

Chapter 3

Labeling

Hewitt, J. P. (1976). *Self and society: A symbolic interactionist social psychology*. Oxford, England: Allyn & Bacon.

Budd, M. A., Hough, S., Wegener, S. T., & Stiers, W. (2017). *Practical psy- chology in medical rehabilitation*. Cham, Switzerland: Springer International Publishing.

http://ksoo.com/a-best-selling-author-overcomes-multiple-disabilities/

https://dictionary.cambridge.org/dictionary/english/reject

https://russiarobinson.wordpress.com/2015/11/05/serial-killer-aileen-wuornos-applying-sociology-theories-to-crime-and-behavior/

Rosenthal, R., & Jacobson, L. (1968). Pygmalion in the classroom. *The Urban Review,* 3(1), 16–20.

https://www.yourdictionary.com/labelling

https://rogercrawford.com/hall-of-fame-speaker/

https://www.collinsdictionary.com/dictionary/english/hall-of-fame

Krohn, M. D., Lizotte, A. J., & Hall, G. P. (Eds.). (2010). *Handbook on crime and deviance*. New York: Springer Science+Business Media.

BSHYNAZ TV $100 TO THE WINNER OF THE RACE. BShynaz Legacy Movement Published on October 7, 2017. https://www.youtube.com/watch?v=vwx5lvypC5Q

https://youtu.be/KrnxCahBJTM

Chapter 4

Confidence & Self esteem

(Self-concept) Plummer, D. (2007). *Self-esteem games for children*. London: Jessica Kingsley Publishers.

Bernard, M. E. (Ed.). (2014). *The strength of self-acceptance: Theory, practice and research*. New York: Springer Science+Business Media.

http://www.businessdictionary.com/definition/self-fulfilling-prophecy.html

Ricciardelli, L. A., & Yager, Z. (2015). *Adolescence and body image: From development to preventing dissatisfaction*. Abingdon: Routledge.

World Health Organization (2019). *Depression*. Retrieved from: https://www.who.int/mental_health/management/depression/en/

https://www.psychologytoday.com/gb/blog/happiness-in-world/201004/the-six-reasons-people-attempt-suicide

Shapiro, Hannah. *Dove's campaign for real beauty boosts girls' self-esteem for back to school*. Examiner.com.

http://www.examiner.com/article/ dove-s-campaign-for-real-beauty-boosts-girls-self-esteem-for-back-to- school

https://www.who.int/en/news-room/fact-sheets/detail/depression

https://www.gov.uk/government/news/new-report-looks-at-the- mental-health-of-children-in-london

Rumination Wyer Jr, R. S. (Ed.). (2013). *Ruminative thoughts: Advances in social cognition* (Vol. 9). New York: Psychology Press.

https://psychologytools.com/what-is-rumination.html

Kinch, John W. (January 1963) A formalized theory of the self-concept. *American Journal of Sociology, 68*(4), 481–486.

https://positivepsychology.com/cbt-cognitive-behavioral-therapy-techniques-worksheets/

Chapter 5

Character

https://hellopoetry.com/words/character/

http://www.dictionary.com/browse/character

https://www.google.co.uk/search?q=what+does+integrity+mean&oq=what

https://dictionary.cambridge.org/dictionary/english/integrity

https://www.youtube.com/watch?v=qabMHmHKJEc

https://www.youtube.com/watch?v=T6QgeLQFdjE

https://www.youtube.com/watch?v=jmXSV_GdvOw

https://dictionary.cambridge.org/dictionary/english/character

https://www.youtube.com/watch?v=GCML561Gl60

Chapter 6

Legacy

https://en.oxforddictionaries.com/definition/legacy

https://www.biography.com/religious-figure/mother-teresa

https://www.britannica.com/biography/Mother-Teresa

https://www.thoughtco.com/the-history-of-apple-computers-1991454

https://www.macmillandictionary.com/dictionary/british/legacy

https://www.collinsdictionary.com/dictionary/english/heavyweight

http://www.oprah.com/own-where-are-they-now/why-muhammad-alis-daughter-laila-ali-stepped-into-the-ring-video

Printed in Great Britain
by Amazon

67392922R00084